CARIBBEAN CREATIVE

A

PLANNER

FOR CREATIVE ENTREPRENEURS

LIVING AND WORKING IN THE CARIBBEAN

by

CECLY ANN MITCHELL

THE WRITERS' WORKSHOPPETT LIMITED

SECOND EDITION

ISBN: 978-976-96362-3-1

Published by:
Les Grand Editeurs Publishers Ltd
61 Old St Joseph Road
Success Village
Laventille
Trinidad.
Email: lesgranediteurs@gmail.com

The Writers' WorkshoppeTT Limited

61 Old St Joseph Road
Success Village
Laventille
Trinidad and Tobago
https://writersworshoppett.webs.com/

FACEBOOK

TABLE OF CONTENTS

NUMBER #1 IN THE KINDLE STORE ON LAUNCH DAY

INTRODUCTION

Very few creatives living and working in commercial fiction in Caribbean can claim the Number ONE spot in Amazon's Kindle store on launch day.

I know two who did, and they are both members of The Writers' WorkshoppeTT Limited.

In a region where Literary fiction rules the roost, this vibrant writing collective based in the Caribbean island nation of Trinidad and Tobago; is focused on producing quality, Caribbean themed, Commercial fiction for international market consumption.

Their members are clearing a table in the global marketplace for home grown Caribbean Commercial fiction in all the popular Genres including Romance, Science Fiction, Fantasy, Mystery, Thrillers, Suspense, and Historical fiction.

As the lead facilitator of The Writers' WorkshoppeTT, I designed this planner for participants of the workshop to plan their literary year.

This planner is the foundation for participants of **The Writers' WorkshoppeTT's** -How-To-Hit that Number ONE spot on launch day- module in the very successful 12-week '**IN YOUR WRITE MIND'** Commercial fiction workshop.

Use it, to define your creative goals for the year.

Here is to your success.

Cecly Ann Mitchell

The Writers WorkshoppeTT Limited

CARIBBEAN CREATIVE

The Road Less Traveled

TAKING A LINE FOR A WALK
WHAT TYPE OF CREATIVE ARE YOU?

In primary schools in the Caribbean, 'Taking A Line for a Walk', was an art exercise used to jump start the creative juices of the students.

Let's use that exercise now, to chart the lifestyle you envision yourself living, as a working artist in the Caribbean.

This is the fun part of this planner.

You get to decide the life you want to live and on what terms.

PLAN POINT - 1

Take a pencil and a blank sheet of paper and let the line wander where it may be on the blank sheet.

Fill each space on the sheet of paper with a creative activity that brings you joy.

List the top three creative activities that bring you joy. The ones you would do for free if the opportunity ever arose.

1.

2.

3.

Have fun.

TAKING A LINE FOR A WALK

PLAN POINT - 1

CREATIVE ENTREPRENEURSHIP

WHAT DO YOU DO?

Now that you have determined the creative activities that bring you joy, narrow the choices down to those activities that you do DAILY.

List all the Creative things you do DAILY and now, approximate how much time you devote to these endeavors on a DAILY basis.

Sorry, my friends, Facebook, Instagram and Snapchat do not count. Neither does Candy Crush.

PLAN POINT - 2

I spend my day creating: (These are examples)

- Artwork

- Novels (Prose or Poetry)

- Music

Have you discovered your niche yet?

No?

Drill deeper to determine the answers to these questions.

How do you allot your hours during the day?

How many hours a day do you spend on the Creative artforms you have listed?

Are you engaged more than 70 hours weekly on these Creative experiences?

Are you spending valuable man-hours creating a commodity that can be sold?

Can you earn a living/wage from your creative endeavors?

PLAN POINT - 2

DAILY ACTIVITIES

PASSION PROJECTS

CREATIVE ENDEAVOURS

CHECKS AND BALANCES

The BALANCE SHEET

Can you see where you are spending valuable man hours creating a commodity, but not appropriating a value to that product?

Let me ask you something.

If you were planning a shopping trip, would you check your wallet before you went to the market, to make your purchases? Or at the counter after you have made your selection?

You would check before you dashed downtown to the store.

It is the same concept you employ, when planning the steps for your Creative career.

Your creative career is not a hobby. It is a business, that keeps a roof over your head, food on the table and pays your medical and other related expenses. You, therefore, as the sole owner, need to take into consideration the resources required to create your commodity.

Too many Caribbean creatives approach their lifestyle without consideration for the vagaries of life.

When there is no plan, your living wage is determined by the marketplace and consumers.

You are the creator. You must know the cost of creating your product and the value that product brings to the market.

No businessperson allows the market to determine the price for their commodity without first determining the cost of production and the value of their competition's commodity in the same marketplace.

As a Creative Entrepreneur working within the Caribbean, you must determine, what VALUE CHAIN your UNIQUE work brings to the landscape of your island.

To do this, you need a Check and Balance spreadsheet.

HERE'S HOW YOU DO THIS

PLAN POINT – 3

Draw up a simple balance sheet. List all your 'expense items' (rent/food/utilities/raw materials/wages/insurance etc.), against the estimated income from your product, you will need to generate over a 12-month period. Add your mark up and distributor's cost and you will have a reasonable value of your product.

CASH PAID OUT	AMOUNT	OTHER OUTCOMES
Advertising		
Commission on sales		
Insurance		
Material and Supplies		
Meals and Entertainment		
Mortgage/Rent		
Office expenses		
Pensions		
Vehicle payments/Transport		
Taxes and Licenses		
Travel Conferences & Workshops		
Utilities		
Wages		
Other Expenses		

CASH RECEIPTS	AMOUNT	OTHER OUTCOMES
Cash Sales		
Returns and allowances		
Donations		
Interest and other income		
Loan proceeds		
Other contributions		

GOALS

What are your Creative Goals for the Creative Year?

PROJECT PLANNER

OBJECTIVE

PLAN OF ACTION

KEY TARGETS

GOALS TO ACHIEVE

ACTION STEPS

KEY PERFORMANCE INDICATORS

FIRST QUARTER

My Goals

1	
2	
3	
4	
5	
6	

Month at a glance
OCTOBER

NOVEMBER

DECEMBER

My Resolutions

SECOND QUARTER

My Goals

1	
2	
3	
4	
5	
6	

Month at a glance
JANUARY

FEBRUARY

MARCH

My Resolutions

THIRD QUARTER

My Goals

1	
2	
3	
4	
5	
6	

Month at a glance
APRIL

MAY

JUNE

My Resolutions

FOURTH QUARTER

My Goals

1	
2	
3	
4	
5	
6	

Month at a glance

JULY

AUGUST

SEPTEMBER

My Resolutions

CREATING YOUR BEST LIFE

YOUR CREATIVE IDEAS

You have done the groundwork. You now know what you create.

How much time you invest in creating the product and what resources and expenses are required to produce the final commodity for market?

It is now time to put action to intent and create the commodity and take that first step to the lifestyle you envisioned for yourself.

1. What's your creative idea?

2. What excites you about this idea?

3. How will bringing this idea to life and completion feel?

4. What will you enjoy about fulfilling this idea?

5. What situations do you have to think through to complete this process?

CREATIVE IDEA

WHAT ARE YOU DOING?

HOW?

DEADLINES = DATES

YOUR CREATIVE PASSION

ALL THE FEELS

1. What excites you?

2. What can you do to prepare mentally for success?

3. What can you do to prepare physically for your success?

SMALL ISLANDS BIG SUCCESS

ONE CARIBBEAN MARKETPLACE

1. Where are you located (what island)?

2. What support structure does your island have specifically for creatives?

3. What can you do to bring awareness to your specific field and brand?

LET'S DO THIS

YOUR AFFIRMATION FOR SUCCESS

This is a contract between your business (self) and your artist (self).

Sign it and stick to the terms.

I _____(Name)_____from the island of

_____(Island)_____will

_____

(insert an actionable commitment to advance your creativity and produce a commodity) to

achieve _____(Goal)_____ by this __/__/20__

Signed,

The Artist

ACCOUNTABILITY

SCHEDULES

PRIORITY SCHEDULE:

MONTH	CREATIVE PROJECT	OUTCOME	
OCTOBER			
NOVEMBER			
DECEMBER			
JANUARY			
FEBRUARY			
MARCH			
APRIL			
MAY			
JUNE			
JULY			
AUGUST			
SEPTEMBER			

MY MUST- DO LIST:

MONTH	TASK
OCTOBER	
NOVEMBER	
DECEMBER	
JANUARY	
FEBRUARY	
MARCH	
APRIL	
MAY	
JUNE	
JULY	
AUGUST	
SEPTEMBER	

SELF-CARE ACTIVITIES

QUARTERLY REVIEW

Use these templates to constantly review your progress

First Quarter	GOAL	OUTCOME	
October			
November			
December			

Second Quarter	GOAL	OUTCOME	
January			
February			
March			

Third Quarter	GOAL	OUTCOME	
April			
May			
June			

Fourth Quarter	GOAL	OUTCOME	
July			
August			
September			

MIDYEAR REVIEW

MONTH	GOAL	OUTCOME	
OCTOBER			
NOVEMBER			
DECEMBER			
JANUARY			
FEBRUARY			
MARCH			

MONTH	GOAL	OUTCOME	
APRIL			
MAY			
JUNE			
JULY			
AUGUST			
SEPTEMBER			

LITERARY CALENDER

CONFERENCES & WORKSHOPS

	MONTH	CONFERENCE
	OCTOBER	
	NOVEMBER	
	DECEMBER	
	JANUARY	
	FEBRUARY	
	MARCH	
	APRIL	
	MAY	
	JUNE	
	JULY	
	AUGUST	
	SEPTEMBER	

	MONTH	WORKSHOP
	OCTOBER	
	NOVEMBER	
	DECEMBER	
	JANUARY	
	FEBRUARY	
	MARCH	
	APRIL	
	MAY	
	JUNE	
	JULY	
	AUGUST	
	SEPTEMBER	

UNITED NATIONS COMMEMORATIVE DAYS

MONTH	COMMEORATIVE DAY
OCTOBER	
NOVEMBER	
DECEMBER	
JANUARY	
FEBRUARY	
MARCH	
APRIL	
MAY	
JUNE	
JULY	
AUGUST	
SEPTEMBER	

If you are a CREATIVE ENTREPRENEUR creating content specifically for events on United Nations Commemorative Days, you may need to record those dates for ease of reference. As an example, March 8th is commemorated annually as International Women's Day.

Visit https://www.un.org/en/sections/observances/international-days/ to record days that are pertinent to your sector.

PERPETUAL CREATIVE CALENDAR

(Input personal days, UN commemorative days and Public holidays)

OCTOBER							NOVEMBER							DECEMBER						
S	M	T	W	T	F	S	S	M	T	W	T	F	S	S	M	T	W	T	F	S

JANUARY							FEBRUARY							MARCH						
S	M	T	W	T	F	S	S	M	T	W	T	F	S	S	M	T	W	T	F	S

APRIL							MAY							JUNE						
S	M	T	W	T	F	S	S	M	T	W	T	F	S	S	M	T	W	T	F	S

JULY							AUGUST							SEPTEMBER						
S	M	T	W	T	F	S	S	M	T	W	T	F	S	S	M	T	W	T	F	S

SETTING UP ACCOUNTS

FOR

PAYMENTS AND ROYALTIES

SETTING UP ACCOUNTS

This section of the planner addresses setting up accounts across all platforms where your creative content will be sold and how, you are paid as a resident of the Caribbean.

Most of the region's nation states have reciprocal tax treaties with the United States, United Kingdom and the European Union and therefore, once your Tax information provided to you by your country of residence is processed you automatically are able to trade on any international platform.

You will need to provide your personal tax information and a local bank account to enable these international platforms to allow you to trade in your sector.

Authors and creators of literature and similar content will discover that there is a plethora of sites where they may upload their content for payment.

However, not all sites offer copyright or content protection.
You are therefore advised to procure necessary instruments of content protection prior to uploading your material on any site, whether they are local or foreign.

THIS SECTION IS CURATED FOR AUTHORPRENEURS

WHAT YOU WILL NEED

1. Individual Tax Number (from your country of residence).
2. ISBN: (INTERNATIONAL IDENTIFIERS)

   Apply through your local ISBN registry for Regional registration. You will need an ISBN for every format of your novel. If you intend to be catalogued on the International marketplace, please contact writersworkshoppett@gmail.com for further instructions.

3. Draft to Digital:

   This is a payment portal for production and distribution to all e-retailers in the USA. You will need to register for an account and pay for their services.

4. Kindle Direct Publishing - Amazon Account:

   Kindle Direct Publishing (KDP) offers a range of options for the Authorpreneur. You will need to register for a KDP account and complete a Tax and financial interviews before your account can be approved.

5. Google Play:

   If you already have a Google account, you can register for the Google Books Partner Programme, to allow your content to be sold and previewed in the Google Play store. Google Books Partner Programme accepts PDFs and eBook formats, which are easily pirated, even with Bowker encrypted ISBNs.

6. Smashwords:

   An accessible, global site, where creators of content can upload their work for payment. Unlike other global content sites, you can upload a Word document to Smashwords, and the platform converts to the format as per your instructions. There is no guarantee that the content you upload will not be pirated.

7. Goodreads

   What is there not to say about Goodreads. Is a platform where authors and readers connect. You cannot have an author account until you have uploaded a novel for publication on one of the store platforms. You can however have a reader account and get acquainted with the platform while you begin your author journey. Your Goodreads author account is linked to an e-retailer platform and this minimizes the threat of content piracy

TO RECEIVE PAYMENT AND ROYALTIES

1. Local Bank account
2. Photo Identification
3. PayPal
4. Payoneer
5. Registration documents as a Sole Trader
6. Registration documents as a Limited Liability Company

PERSONAL NOTES

WORKING SCHEDULE

YOUR WORKING SCHEDULE

As a Creative Entrepreneur you need to establish a regular creative working schedule. Obviously, you need to create, but you also need to manage the administrative side of your growing Creative business.

Apart from the business of producing a commodity, you will need to manage registration of identities, financial institutions, managing Identifiers, procurement of raw material and other supplies, markets (physical and online), marketing, the whole works. Remember, there also will be Social Media content to create, upload and manage in a timely manner.

You therefore as a Creative Entrepreneur need to manage your time, to give you the opportunity to create content that is relevant and meets the expectations of your audience and consumers.

A schedule is not just for creating.
It is putting time aside every day to focus on your business of creating. It is taking your creativity out of the hobby column and firmly placing it in the 'this keeps the roof over my head, food on the table, clothes on my back, and teeth in my mouth' column.

SKILLS PAY THE BILLS
WORK SCHEDULE

MORNINGS	
9:00	
9:30	
10:00	
10:30	
11:00	
11:30	

LUNCH	
12:00	
12:30	
1:00	
1:30	

AFTERNOON	
2:00	
2:30	
3:00	
3:30	
4:00	
4:30	

NOTES

NOTE FROM THE AUTHOR

The Facilitator
Of
The Writers' WorkshoppeTT Limited

Thank you for purchasing 'Caribbean Creative Entrepreneur Planner'.

This workbook contains templates to help the creative person, resident in the Caribbean, define the value chain of their sector to enable them to earn a living wage from their creative endeavors. The book was designed specifically to help members of The Writers' WorkshoppeTT plan their Literary year (October 1st- September 30th), and focus on achieving their publishing targets for that period.

The Writers' WorkshoppeTT is a collective of Trinidad and Tobago authors, writing Commercial fiction for the global audience.

Caribbean Creative Entrepreneur Planner is designed to help those authors plan their Literary Year, with emphasis on the consistent creation and timely release of content for the Commercial fiction market.

As I indicated in the Introduction of this book, novels written by two of our members launched in the Number 1 spot in the Amazon Kindle store for New releases in the Caribbean and Latin American category on September 30th, 2019.

It is anticipated that within the Literary Year, members will continue to dominate Amazon's new release charts for Commercial fiction within this region.

This paperback edition of Caribbean Creative does not include all that we do to take our authors to the coveted Number 1 position. You must be a part of our workshop to have that experience. However, I have included the first section of 'In Your Write Mind', workbook to give you a little idea of what we do.

Thank you
Cecly Ann Mitchell

IN YOUR WRITE MIND

IN YOUR WRITE MIND

COMMERCIAL FICTION
WORKBOOK
SERIES

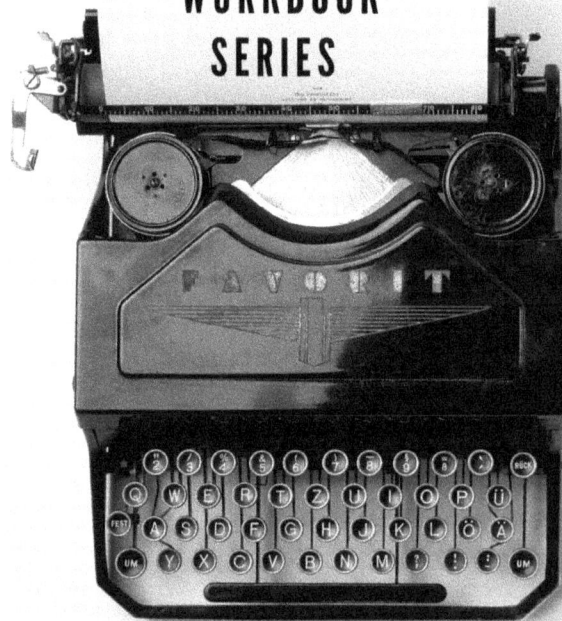

FAVORIT

CECLY ANN MITCHELL
THE WRITERS' WORKSHOPPETT

Price $100 (TT)
Order your copies at
writersworkshoppett@gmail.com

NOT AVAILABLE IN BOOKSHOPS OR ONLINE

SECTION 1

INTRODUCTION TO COMMERCIAL FICTION

WHAT IS COMMERCIAL FICTION

In response to this workshop, someone wrote that Commercial fiction was not their genre. What is Commercial fiction?

In general, fiction is divided into Literary fiction (which is predominant here in the Caribbean) and Commercial fiction (also known as genre or mainstream fiction). Because I want you to understand the major differences I'm going to spend two minutes explaining to you the difference between what you are attempting to write and the work of the various West Indian novelists that you have read.

Pick any West Indian novelist with which we are familiar.

Vidia Naipaul, Samuel Selvon, Ralph de Boissiere, George Lamming, Marlon James, Lawrence Scott, Earl Lovelace, Joanne Hillhouse, Edwidge Danticat, Merle Hodge, Marlon James, Kei Miller, they all write Literary fiction.

There are basic differences, and those differences affect how the book is read, packaged, and marketed.

Basically **Literary fiction** usually centres around a timeless, complex theme, and rarely has a fulfilling resolved or happy ending. Think about novels by Vida Naipaul, and Toni Morrison. Literary fiction is usually more concerned with style and characterization and is also usually paced more slowly than commercial fiction.

Commercial fiction, on the other hand, is faster paced, with a stronger definitive, plot (more events, higher stakes, more dangerous situations). Characterization is generally not as central to the story. The theme is very obvious, and the narrative (language) not as complex.

The biggest difference between literary and commercial fiction is that editors expect to make a substantial profit from selling a commercial book, but not necessarily from selling literary fiction. Audiences for commercial fiction are larger than those for literary fiction.

Think about all the novelists that you read:

- Brenda Jackson
- Beverly Jenkins
- James Patterson,
- J. K. Rowling
- George Martin
- Danielle Steel
- Tom Clancy
- Stephen King
- John Grisham
- Marie Force
- Ana E Ross
- Farrah Rochon
- Jamaica Kincaid
- Nalo Hopkinson

are all examples of Commercial fiction authors.

One of the easiest ways to determine whether your work is literary or commercial is to ask yourself, "Is my book more likely to be read in college English classes, or in the grocery checkout line?"

So now that we understand what Commercial fiction is from the perspective of a reader, let's break it down to what you write, or what you want to write.

This is where your notebooks and your trusted pencils, come into play.

SHOW US YOUR STORY IDEA

WHO is your main character?	
WHAT happens to him or her?	
WHERE does it happen?	
WHY does it happen?	
HOW does it end?	

For the purpose of Commercial fiction, the What, the Why and the How are pivotal to the development of the story.

Commercial fiction is PLOT driven and there must be a resolution.

There must be internal and external change to your main character at the resolution of the story.

NOTES

NOTES

THE WRITERS' WORKSHOPPETT LIMITED

WORKSHOP SCHEDULE

IN YOUR WRITE MIND: 12-week Commercial fiction workshop

for aspiring authors of all levels serious about writing commercial fiction.

Learn to:
Plot and structure your novel to suit the genre.
Delve into the key elements of POV, Beats, and Voice.
Write a succinct Synopsis and query letter for your submissions.
Decipher the economics of writing full time and writing work that sells.
email: writersworkshoppett@gmail.com
Include your name and a contact number in the body of the email.

VENUE: ONLINE

IN YOUR WRITE MIND – COMMERCIAL FICTION

MONDAYS 10 am – 12 noon

WRITE ME A STORY – WRITING FOR CHILDREN

TUESDAYS 10 am- 12 noon

REALITY WRITES - MEMOIR WRITING

THURSDAYS 10 am – 12 noon

IN YOUR WRITE MIND – COMMERCIAL FICTION

SATURDAYS 10 am – 12 noon

~~~~~~~

THE WRITERS' WORKSHOPPETT LIMITED

THE WRITERS' WORKSHOPPETT

ANNUAL MEMBERSHIP

$240.00 TT

LITERARY YEAR
OCTOBER 1ST - SEPTEMBER 30TH

The Writers' WorkshoppeTT is an organization dedicated to providing a unique writing experience for writers, resident in Trinidad and Tobago and the wider Caribbean who are seeking success as Commercial fiction authors.

www.ingramcontent.com/pod-product-compliance
Lightning Source LLC
Chambersburg PA
CBHW081422270326
41931CB00015B/3375